THE FRED FACTOR

"**Mark Sanborn is a phenomenal speaker and an outstanding storyteller.** This work is a superb extension of his wisdom and substance. It'll only take you a few minutes to read but it's guaranteed to give you a lifetime of value. Enjoy the book and share it with everyone in your organization for maximum benefit."

—Nido R. Qubein
Chairman, Great Harvest Bread Company
Founder, National Speakers Association Foundation
Author, *Stairway to Success*

"Goodness is in shorter supply than is necessary. *The Fred Factor* is a book about how all of us can add to the goodness in the world through simple daily acts that touch the lives of others. This is good for you and also good for your business. People are starving for genuine human attention. Become a Fred, eliminate the shortage, and have a great time doing so."

—Jim Cathcart
Author, *Relationship Selling*
and *The Acorn Principle*

"*The Fred Factor* is the perfect one-hour read. You cannot finish it without feeling compelled go the extra mile for others and just plain be a better person."

—Jimmy Calano
Cofounder and former CEO, CareerTrack

THE FRED FACTOR

EVERY PERSON'S GUIDE TO MAKING THE ORDINARY
EXTRAORDINARY!

MARK SANBORN

**Executive
Books**

THE FRED FACTOR

Published by
Executive Books
206 West Allen Street
Mechanicsburg, PA 17055

Copyright © 2002 by Mark Sanborn

ISBN: 0-937539-62-7

LCCN: 2002107245

Printed in the United States of America

Cover design by David M. Bullock/Susquehanna Direct

06 05 04   5 4 3 2

Contents

Contents

1 The First Fred I Ever Met

> *Make each day your masterpiece.*
>
> Joshua Wooden,
> John Wooden's Father

The first time I met a "Fred" was just after I had purchased what I called a "new old house." Located in a beautiful, tree-lined area of Denver called Washington Park, the house had been built in 1928. A first-time homeowner, I'd only been living there for a few days when I heard a knock on my front door. I opened it, and saw a mailman standing there.

"Good morning, Mr. Sanborn!" he exclaimed cheerfully. "My name is Fred and I'm your postal carrier. I just stopped by to introduce myself, welcome you to the neighborhood and find out a little bit about you and what you do for a living." Of medium height and build with a small mustache, Fred was an ordinary-looking fellow. But, while his physical appearance didn't convey anything out of the ordinary, his sincerity and warmth were noticeable immediately.

I was taken aback. I'd been receiving mail for most of my life, but I had never received anything like this kind of an introduction from my postal carrier. But it did impress me as a nice touch.

I replied, "I'm a professional speaker. I don't have a real job."

"If you're a professional speaker, you must travel a

7

lot," said Fred.

"Yes, I do. I travel anywhere from 160 to 200 days a year."

Nodding, Fred went on. "Well, if you just give me a copy of your schedule, I'll hold your mail and bundle it. I'll only deliver it on the days that you are at home to receive it."

This was amazing! But, as I told Fred, that was probably not necessary. "Why not just leave the mail in the box on the side of the house?" I suggested. "Then I'll pick it up when I came back into town."

Fred explained, "Mr. Sanborn, burglars often watch for mail building up in a box. That tells them that you're out of town, and you might become the victim of a break-in."

Fred was more worried about my mail then I was! But after all, I realized, he was the postal professional.

He continued, "Here's what I suggest. I can put mail in your box as long as the lid closes. That way nobody will know that you're gone. Whatever doesn't fit in the box, I'll put between the screen door and the front door. Nobody can see it there. And if that area becomes too full of mail, I'll just hold the rest of it for you until you come back into town."

At this point I started to wonder: does this guy really work for the U.S. Postal Service? Maybe this neighborhood had its own private mail delivery service. Still, Fred's suggestions sounded like a terrific plan to me, so I agreed to them.

Two weeks later I returned home from a trip. As I put the key in my front door lock, I noticed that my doormat was missing. I was puzzled; I doubted that anyone was actually stealing doormats in Denver. I looked around on my front porch and I found my doormat in the corner. It was covering something.

Here's what had happened: While I was gone, UPS had misdelivered a package sent to me. The box was left on somebody else's porch five doors down. Lucky for me, Fred the Postman was on the job.

Noticing my box on the wrong porch, he picked it up, carried it down to my house and put it out of view. He also attached a note explaining what had happened, and then tried to make it less noticeable by placing the doormat over it.

Not only was Fred delivering the mail, he was now picking up slack for UPS!

His actions really struck me. As a professional speaker, it is easy to find and point out what's "wrong" with quality, customer service and business in general. Finding examples of what's "right," or even praiseworthy, is much harder. Yet here was Fred, a gold-plated example of what personalized service looked like and a role model for anyone who wanted to make a difference in his or her work.

Because of Fred's example, I started sharing my experiences with him in speeches and seminars I presented across the country. Everyone, it seemed, wanted to hear about Fred, whether they were in a service business or manufacturing, high tech or healthcare. Audiences were enthralled and inspired.

Back at home, sometimes I had a chance to share with Fred how his work was inspiring others. I told him about a discouraged employee who had been receiving no recognition from her employers. She wrote to tell me that Fred's example inspired her to "keep on keeping on" and doing what she knew in her heart was the right thing to do, regardless of recognition or reward.

I related the confession of a manager who pulled me aside after one speech to tell me he never realized that his career goal all along was to be "a Fred." He believed in excellence and quality as the goal of every person in any business or profession.

And I was delighted to tell him that several companies created a Fred Award to present to employees who demonstrated the same spirit of service, innovation and commitment that he did.

Someone once sent Fred a box of homemade cookies, care of my address!

As for myself, I wanted to thank Fred more formally for his exceptional service. When Christmas rolled around, I left a small gift in the mailbox for him. The next day, when the mail was delivered, I found an unusual letter in my box. The envelope had a stamp on it, but the stamp wasn't canceled. That's when I noticed the return address. The letter was from Fred the Postman.

Fred knew it was illegal to put a letter that wasn't posted in the box. So, even though he personally carried it from his house to my house, he still put a stamp on to keep it legal.

The letter said, in part, "Dear Mr. Sanborn, Thank you for remembering me at Christmas... I am flattered you talk about me in your speeches and seminars. I hope I can continue to provide exceptional service. Sincerely, Fred the Postman."

Over the next ten years, I received consistently

remarkable service from Fred. I could always tell the days when he wasn't working my street just by the way the mail was jammed in my box. When Fred was on the job it was always neatly bundled.

But Fred also took a personal interest in me. One day, while I was mowing the front lawn, a vehicle slowed in the street. The window went down and a familiar voice yelled, "Hello, Mr. Sanborn! How was your trip?"

It was Fred, off duty and driving around the neighborhood.

To this day, I can't tell you what motivated Fred. I know he didn't get paid more for his extraordinary work. I doubt he received any special recognition from his employer (if he did, I never heard about it). I know he wasn't privy to any exceptional training or incentive programs.

One thing I do know: Fred, and the way he did his job, is a perfect metaphor for anyone who wants to achieve and excel in the 21st century. Truth is transferable, and the four principles I learned from Fred apply to any person in any profession.

Principle #1: Everyone makes a difference.

It doesn't matter how large or even how screwed up an organization is. An individual can still make a difference within that organization. An employer can hinder exceptional performance, choose to ignore it, and not adequately recognize or encourage it. Or, an employer can train employees to achieve exceptional performance and then reward it. But ultimately, only the employee can choose to do his or her job in an extraordinary way, either because of, or in spite of, circumstances.

The Fred Factor

Think about it. Do you add to or take away from the experience of your customers and colleagues? Do you move your organization closer to or further from its goals? Do you perform your work in an ordinary way or do you execute it superbly? Do you lighten someone's burden, or add to it? Do you lift someone up, or put someone down?

Nobody can prevent you from choosing to be exceptional. The only question at the end of the day that matters is, "What kind of difference do you make?"

Fred Smith, the distinguished author and business leader, has noted from his years of leadership experience that, "Most people have a passion for significance."

I agree. Consider what Fred did. He delivered mail. Where others might have seen monotony and drudgery, he saw an opportunity to make a greater difference in the lives of others. And a positive difference is what he made.

Martin Luther King said, "If a man is called to be a street sweeper, he should sweep streets even as Michelangelo painted or Beethoven composed music or Shakespeare wrote poetry. He should sweep streets so well that all the hosts of heaven and earth will pause to say, 'Here lived a great street sweeper who did his job well.'"

Fred understood this. He is proof that there are no insignificant or ordinary jobs when they're performed by significant and extraordinary people. Politicians are fond of telling us that work gives people dignity. I don't disagree. Having work to do, and the means to make a living for one's self and family, is important. But that is only half of the equation.

What we haven't been told nearly enough is that people give work dignity. There are no unimportant jobs, just people who feel unimportant in their jobs. That's probably why B.C. Forbes, the legendary founder of Forbes magazine, said, "There is more credit and satisfaction in being a first-rate truck driver than a tenth-rate executive."

I have personally met a cab driver or two more inspired in how they performed their work than some upper level managers who seemed to have lost any inspiration for excellence. Still, while position never determines performance, ultimately performance determines position in life. That's because position is based on results, rather than intentions. It's about actually doing what others usually only talk about.

Setting a higher standard is more challenging than simply achieving the status quo. Ignoring the criticism of those who are threatened by the achievement of others depends not on your title, but on your attitude. Ultimately, the more value you create for others, the more value will eventually flow towards you. Knowing you've done your best, independent of the support, acknowledgement or reward of others, is a key determinant in a fulfilling career.

Principle #2: Success is built on relationships.

Most of the mail sent to me has ended up in my mailbox. The service was performed by the U.S. Postal Service, which gave me what I paid for—nothing more, nothing less. In contrast, the service I received from Fred was amazing for many reasons, but the biggest reason was the relationship I had with Fred. It differed from the relationships I've had with any other postal carrier, before or since. As a matter of fact, Fred was probably the only postal carrier I felt I ever had a personal relationship with.

It's easy to see why. Indifferent people deliver impersonal service. Service becomes personalized when a relationship exists between the provider and the customer. Fred took time to get to know me and to understand my needs and preferences. And then he used that information to provide better service than I had ever received before.

Fred is proof that, in any job or business, relationship building is the most important objective, because the quality of the relationship determines the quality of the product or service. That's also why:

● Leaders succeed when they recognize the human nature of their employees.
● Technology succeeds when it recognizes the human nature of its users.
● Fred the Postman still succeeds because he recognizes the human nature of his work.

Principle #3: You must continually create value for others and it doesn't have to cost a penny.

Don't have enough money? The necessary training? The right opportunities? In other words, do you ever complain that you lack resources? Have you started believing that "more with less" is an impossibility?

Then consider Fred. What resources did he have at his disposal? A drab blue uniform and a bag. That's it! He walked up and down streets with that bag full of mail, and his heart and head full of imagination. That imagination enabled him to create value for his customers, and he didn't spend an extra dollar to do it. He just thought a little bit harder and more creatively than most other postal carriers.

In doing so, Fred mastered what I believe is the most important job skill of the 21st century: the ability to create value for customers without spending more money to do it. You, too, can replace money with imagination. The object is to outthink your competition rather than outspend them.

Over the years, I've met many people who were concerned that they might lose their jobs and become victims of downsizing. They were worried about whether or not they would be employed in the months ahead.

I always tell them to quit worrying about it. That usually gets their attention. Of course, they are shocked at what seems to be my indifference. In reality, I am just trying to refocus their attention from being employed to being employable.

A high school or college graduate today can probably count on being unemployed a few times during his or her career. But that unemployment will be brief, as long as the individual is employable. To be employable means having a skill set that makes a person desirable to any employer, regardless of industry or geographic location.

So what makes someone employable? There are many skills that contribute to employability, but I am convinced that the most critical skill is this: the ability to create value for customers and colleagues without spending money to do it. The trick is to replace money with imagination, to substitute creativity for capital.

Sanborn's Maxim says that the faster you try to solve a problem with money, the less likely it is the best solution. Anyone can buy his or her way out of a problem with enough money. The challenge is to outthink, rather than to outspend, the competition.

This raises an interesting question: just what competition did Fred face? For many of us in the world of business, the competition is either inside or outside our organizations, and sometimes both. For example, you may be competing for a better position in your department or company. While professional decorum might prevent you from describing it this way, you hope that the best man or woman for the job will be the one who gets it, and you're working to prove that you're that person.

Often there is an identified competitor in the marketplace, too. When I spoke at a conference cosponsored by a delivery service that considers the U.S. Postal Service a rival, I was forbidden to use the story of Fred in my presentation. (It struck me as odd that the company wouldn't want me to use Fred as an example of the kind of service it aspired to and encouraged all of their employees to deliver.)

Because the Postal Service competes for revenue against alternative carriers, employees like Fred can help or hinder the cause. Most employers recognize that Fred is the kind of employee who could give them a competitive advantage, whether or not Fred thought in those terms.

I'm not sure that he does. I think Fred is proof that there is another, less tangible competitor in the world. That competitor is the job we could have done. In a manner of speaking, we compete against our potential every day. And most of us, myself included, fall short of what we are capable of doing or being.

I don't assume to understand all that motivates Fred, but I suspect the gratification he gets from excelling in his work is a big factor, as are the happiness and service he consistently delivers to his customers.

But, at the end of the day, Fred has beaten a silent opponent that threatens his potential, just as it threatens yours and mine. That competitor is mediocrity, a willingness to do just enough and nothing more than necessary to get by.

And while this competitor may not beat you out for a

job promotion or take away corporate market share, it will just as surely diminish the quality of your performance and the meaning you derive from it.

Principle #4: You can reinvent yourself regularly.

The most important lesson I've learned from Fred begs a question: If Fred could bring such originality to putting mail in a box, how much more could you and I reinvent our work?

There are days when you wake up tired. You figure you've read the books, listened to the audiotapes, watched the videos, and sat through the training sessions. You're doing everything you can possibly do but you're still fatigued and unmotivated. So when life is at low tide—when your professional commitment is wavering and just getting the job done and going home at the end of the day becomes your primary objective—what do you do?

Here's what I do: I think about the guy who used to deliver my mail. Because if Fred the Postman could bring that kind of creativity and commitment to putting mail in a box, I can do as much or more to reinvent my work and rejuvenate my efforts. I believe that no matter what job you hold, what industry you work in or where you live, every morning you wake up with a tabula rasa, a clean slate. You can make your business, as well as your life, anything you choose it to be.

A New Way to Work

Inspired by Fred the Postman and the countless other Freds I've met, observed or been served by in numerous professions, I put together The Fred Factor. It contains the simple yet profound lessons all the Freds taught me. Anyone can do them. Everyone should. By learning how to be a Fred, it's possible to do extraordinary work. And that means being an extraordinary person as well—something we all want to be.

2 Freds are Everywhere

> *There comes a special moment in everyone's life, a moment for which that person was born. That special opportunity, when he seizes it, will fulfill his mission—a mission for which he is uniquely qualified. In that moment, he finds greatness. It is his finest hour.*
>
> Winston Churchill

I love Starbucks coffee. I rarely start my day without it. One morning, as I was driving to Denver's International Airport, I swung by Starbucks for a grande, a really large cup of steaming coffee.

Back on the interstate in the Mitsubishi Eclipse, I realized that I was in a bit of a dilemma. The car didn't have an automatic shift, which meant that I needed one hand to shift and, of course, the other to drive. I set my coffee down on the center console for a moment. What were the odds that the coffee would spill?

The odds were in the coffee's favor. Suddenly, a dark hot stain spread all over my right leg, from my knee up to my hip. And I was wearing LIGHT BLUE jeans. At the airport I applied some jean first aid by squeegeeing my pants and using the rest room hand dryer. But I still looked like a giant dork.

As soon as I checked into the Airport Marriott in Atlanta, I called housekeeping. "These coffee-stained jeans

18

are the only pants I have to wear for my return trip home," I explained to the supervisor. "Is there any chance I can get them washed overnight?"

With a lot of sympathy in her voice she informed me that not only was there no guest laundry, but the crew that washed linens had gone for the day. But she informed me that she would be glad to pick up my jeans, take them home and wash them and return them early the next morning.

Needless to say, I agreed.

The next morning this incredible woman delivered a clean pair of freshly washed—and pressed—jeans to my door.

I still regret that I didn't write down her name (although I did write a glowing letter about her to the hotel). But even though I can't recall her given name, I know who she was.

She was a Fred.

Freds are Everywhere You Go

Ever since I met Fred the Postman, I've been aware that Freds are all over the place. The more of them I see, the more I realize that they are a lot less the exception to the rule than I thought. Not only that—each one is truly an individual in his or her own way.

Funny Fred

Passengers on the 6:15 am flight from Denver to San Francisco are rarely at their perkiest. From experience, I know the flight can be a sleeping, uneventful one. Of course, it depends on which flight attendant is on the airplane intercom.

The Fred Factor

On one flight that I took, the passengers were treated to some unorthodox announcements from the flight attendant who had been working the first-class cabin.

"If you are having a hard time getting your ears to pop, I suggest you yawn widely," she began. "And if you are having a hard time yawning, ask me and I'll tell you about my love life.

"We are on final approach into San Francisco airport. If San Francisco is your final destination, I hope you'll have a safe drive home. There is some blockage on the northbound 405 and it appears there is a stalled car at the Market Street exit. But otherwise, traffic appears to be moving smoothly."

The usually sleepy passengers were waking up; there was laughter throughout the airplane. But there was more to come. After touching down, the flight attendant was back with final instructions.

"Unless the person next to you has beaten me to it, let me be the first to welcome you to San Francisco. You'll notice that the airport buildings are in the distance. We don't land at the terminal because it scares the heck out of the people inside. That's why we land way out here. That means we'll need to taxi, so please don't stand up until we are parked at the gate and the seat belt sign has been turned off.

"For those of you who are 1Ks, Premiers and frequent fliers—there are too many of you on board to mention by name, but you know who you are—we thank you for choosing United for your extensive travels. And if you'll leave me a recent picture as you deplane, I'll be glad to mail it to your loved ones so that they remember what you look like.

"My final hope is that when you leave the airplane, you'll do so with a big smile on your face. That way the people outside will wonder just what it is we do up here in the friendly skies."

Here's what this Fred did: She took some risks and had some fun. As a result, the passengers—or rather, her "customers"—had fun, too.

An Accountable Fred

Jack Foy works as a night auditor at Homewood Suites in Worthington, Ohio. One evening, a woman whose husband was staying at the property called with a special request. For Father's Day, the man's daughter wanted to make sure that her dad had his favorite breakfast of pancakes, eggs and bacon.

The only problem is that Homewood Suites doesn't have a restaurant. So at 7:00 AM, when Jack got off work, he drove to a nearby restaurant to pick up the special meal. He also bought a card and used a crayon to sign it "From Daddy's Little Girl." Then he drove back to the hotel and delivered the care package to one very astonished and grateful guest.

Oh, and by the way, that act of service resulted in a huge contract for Jack's hotel. Value-added accounting: now that's Fred Power!

A Generous Fred

I had just checked into the Crown Plaza in Columbus, Ohio, when I discovered that I didn't have enough cash to catch a cab back to the airport the next morning. The person at the front desk told me that the hotel couldn't advance me any cash on my American Express card. I was, however, informed that some cabs did take credit cards. Unfortunately, I was scheduled to end my speech at 9:00 and I wanted to catch a 9:40 flight. I was afraid that the additional time required to line up am accommodating cab, along with the accompanying paperwork, would make it even more difficult to make my flight.

My troubles didn't end there. I found that my room key didn't work so I headed down the hall to the house phone which was located directly outside the clubroom. The man on duty in the clubroom noticed that I was making a call and that I still had all my luggage. "Is there a problem?" he inquired, introducing himself as Nick. I explained that my room key wouldn't work. "I'll take care of it," he said and then asked, "Would you like a drink on me for your inconvenience?" I requested a beer and ate some snacks while Nick called for a new key to be brought up.

Nick was so helpful that, once I had my key, I decided to share my embarrassing dilemma with him. He listened and then said, "If all else fails, check back with me and I'll take care of it." He informed me that he was on duty until 7:30 the next morning and asked, "Shall I call you to make sure you have the money you need before I leave?" I told him that that would be very thoughtful.

Finally in my room, I spent the next forty minutes on the phone with my office, my bank and American Express. I had an ATM card but I'd never used it and didn't have the pin number memorized. My "personal banker" said there was nothing she could do. American Express could provide cash, but the information they had about my bank was thirteen years out of date! I'd have to call home, hope to catch my wife, get the new bank account information and call them back. Then I'd have to find an American Express ATM machine. My office manager, Mary Ellen, came up with several possible solutions, but even her resourcefulness failed to help me get the money I needed. I decided to go back to Nick.

Freds are Everywhere

"This is embarrassing, Nick," I confessed. "I've traveled all over the world and ran out of money only twice in twenty years. I hate to ask but can I borrow $20 from you?"

Without a moment's hesitation, Nick replied, "No problem! These things happen." Opening his wallet, he offered, "Here, take $30." I tried to explain that I only needed $20.

"No, no, take the $30," he insisted. "You never know what might come up." We exchanged addresses and I promised to send him the money as soon as I arrived home.

I was both gratified and stunned by Nick's generous assistance. A problem that couldn't be expediently solved by American Express, Norwest Bank, or even my own office was worked out by one helpful individual who was willing to be of service.

Thirty dollars isn't a lot of money, but neither is it a little money, especially when it comes out of one's pocket. Nick had never seen me before and, for all he knew, he would never see or hear from me again. He understood the risks associated with truly being of service and still he was willing to accept them.

When I returned to my office the next day, I mailed Nick a check along with some of my books and tapes to express my appreciation.

Has Nick ever been stiffed? Has he ever helped out a guest who either failed to appreciate or repay him? I don't know, and I'm speculating now, but my sense of him is that he will continue to be of service, even if those he helps don't always repay him.

I believe that because I believe that Nick knows. He knows that the way to move through life joyfully and successfully is by focusing on what you give rather than what you get. He knows that you don't just do the right thing because you have to do it. You do it because it is the right thing to do. Nick knows that being of service isn't an obligation, but an opportunity. He knows that being helpful is even more fun than being helped.

What an important reminder! It is kind of funny, but I'm actually glad that I ran out of money because I got to meet Nick and be reminded of what Nick knows. And because of that, you and I now know, too.

Other Freds Who Know

A waitress had just finished her shift at Morton's of Chicago. As she was walking to her car, she recognized a man in the parking lot as a guest she had served earlier in the evening. He was struggling, quite unsuccessfully, to change the flat tire on his car. "Let me help," she offered. In short order, this enterprising waitress had been of even greater service to the restaurant patron and he was on his way.

On a flight to Orlando, the fun-loving steward put on a Goofy cap and invited the children to join him in the front of the cabin where he did magic tricks for them. A flight attendant on the same flight sat on the floor with a child in her lap, giving a frazzled parent a much-needed break from childcare.

At Crested Butte Mountain Ski Resort, an employee repaired a skier's disabled car in the parking lot. Another used his own permit to cut a tree after work so a family that was staying at the resort would have a Christmas tree for their holiday vacation.

A cable installer in southern California does a lot more than his official job description. He programs the remote switcher for the new channels, sets the timer on the VCR and often improves sound quality by repositioning the stereo antenna and speakers.

A few months ago, a friend of mine went to the movies and forgot her wallet. When she asked an employee if she could write a check she was told not to worry about it. Instead, she was asked to drop the money off the next time she was nearby. After she got her seat, the same employee who waved her into the theater brought her a box of popcorn and a soft drink. How often does she go to that movie theater? Every chance she gets.

Once I had a particularly unpleasant experience trying to get home to Denver from Philadelphia. The airline personnel I encountered at the airport seemed unable or unwilling to help, so I called the toll-free number for frequent fliers and requested a supervisor. She was genuinely empathic and went to great lengths to make sure I was booked on a flight back to Denver that night. Her hard work was greatly appreciated, but even more impressive was this: she called my office the next day to make sure that I'd made it home okay!

Freds Understand Their Clients

Both capitation, the limits that HMOs put on providers for care, and managed care have changed the way healthcare is delivered. What hasn't changed is the human input. There are still extraordinary healthcare workers who focus on what they can do instead of what they can't. With all the complaining about healthcare, you might not expect to find a stellar example of Fred in this field.

Dan, a physician's assistant, is a Fred. Imagine working in a practice that specializes in kids. The only thing tougher than treating a sick adult is treating a sick child.

The Fred Factor

I wasn't there the day my wife, Darla, took our three year-old son in for an examination. We wanted to be sure that a fall on the grandparents' coffee table hadn't dislocated his jawbone. Hunter was sitting on the floor when Dan came in. After a cheerful greeting, Dan plopped down on the floor next to him.

Hunter watched suspiciously while snacking on pretzels. "Hey dude, can I have one?" asked Dan. Children learn very quickly to recognize their environments, and after a few visits to any doctor's office, most kids find themselves leery at least terrified at worst. So it wasn't surprising when Hunter's eyes got a little bigger as Dan brazenly reached out and took a pretzel from the bag.

Suddenly, a big smile broke across my son's face. Dan proceeded to "interact" in medical terms (in normal language, he and Hunter played). They wrestled and goofed around—and Dan tied Hunter's shoelaces together. When Hunter saw this he tried to walk and, predictably, tripped. He loved it and laughed with glee.

After several minutes of frivolity, Dan was able to examine a totally stress-free little boy. Hunter probably thought he'd misjudged and wasn't really in a medical facility after all.

Dan, on the other hand (or foot) knew what do. He not only performed his examination with a minimum of fuss—he actually eliminated fear from a three-year old.

Now that's Fred thinking at its best. But, lest you think that Freds are anonymous people, let me share another Fred story.

Freds are Everywhere

A Famous Fred

Finding a summer job in the Bronx in the early 1950s wasn't easy, but young Colin was determined to earn the money he needed. He showed up early every morning at the Teamsters Hall to volunteer for day jobs. Sometimes he landed a spot on a soda delivery truck as a helper. Then a job cleaning up sticky soda syrup opened up at a Pepsi plant. None of the other kids volunteered, but Colin did. And he did such a good job that he was invited back the following summer. That time, he operated a bottling machine instead of a mop. By the end of that second summer, he was a deputy shift leader.

It taught him an important lesson. "All work is honorable," he wrote in his memoir, "Always do your best because someone is watching."

Years later, the world watched as Colin Powell served as the Chairman of the Joint Chiefs of Staff, lead the military effort in the Gulf War and established himself as a champion of education. In 2000, he was chosen by President-elect George W. Bush as Secretary of State.

Freds, indeed, are everywhere.

3 How to be a Fred

Ever find yourself saying, "I wish I knew, lived and worked with more people like Fred the Postman!"? We would all benefit from a world populated by people like Fred—people who take that kind of pride in their work and turn the ordinary into the extraordinary.

Question: How can we get more Freds in the world?

Answer: Be A Fred!

How many "Freds" are in your organization? Have you ever found yourself saying, "I wish we had more people like that around here!"? Do you regret that some of your team-mates might more accurately be described as "the anti-Freds?"

It all starts with you. If you want more Freds, *be* a Fred. Only when *you* make the ordinary extraordinary will others see the possibilities for themselves.

It isn't hard. Actually, it's harder not to be a Fred. The skills and abilities that enable us to make the ordinary truly extraordinary are natural; they come out of who we already are. If you didn't have at least an interest (or more likely, a burning desire) to make the most of your career and rela-tionships, you wouldn't have made it this far into the book.

If there is one thing that unites us all, it is this: a pas-sion for significance. I've never met anyone who wanted to be insignificant. Everyone wants to count, to know that what he or she does each day isn't simply a means of making a liv-ing, but a living of making meaning. The unhappiest people of all may well be those who go to jobs they hate because they need the money. Why not go to a job you love because you need the money?

You can. Convert your job into one you love, not by doing a different job, but by doing the one you have differently!

That's what made Fred unique. Thousands of men and women deliver the mail. For some, it is "just a job." For many it may be an occupation they enjoy. But for a few like Fred, delivering the mail becomes a calling.

The person doing the work determines the difference between the mundane and the magnificent.

You Choose

Which do you prefer, enjoyment or misery? Feeling good about your work, or feeling bad about it? Being yourself, or hiding whom you really are? It is harder to be miserable, negative and insincere than to be happy, positive and genuine. All Freds share those latter characteristics, no matter what type of work they do.

Most people think they get ahead in life by learning something new. I believe you can also get ahead by going back to the basics of success. There are lots of ways to define true success, but I believe that having the most fun doing your best work is at the top of the list.

All it takes is reestablishing what you've always known—and probably learned in kindergarten or Sunday school—and start reapplying it.

The Fred Factor
Do the Right Thing for the Right Reason

Here's a mystery: if you expect praise and recognition, oddly, it will seldom come. I really don't know why, but life has demonstrated repeatedly that if your motive for doing something is to get thanked or praised for what you've done, you'll often be disappointed. If, however, you go about doing the right thing knowing that the doing is it's own reward, you'll be fulfilled whether or not you get recognition from others. When reward or recognition comes, it will be icing on an already delectable cake.

Your Possibilities are Endless

Here's my take on why people love to hear the story of Fred the Postman: it reminds them of what is possible. Excellence, wisdom and dedication are all functioning parts of Fred's world. The mediocrity, foolishness and lack of commitment we encounter every day seem poor substitutes.

Fred is a reminder that we can choose the right role models. Freds set an inspiring example for their companies and organizations, teammates and customers. When others see the infinite ways to create excellence and "wow" in their work, then they, too, will want to become Freds.

Then something wonderful will happen. The energy they once had will be restored. Enthusiasm will replace cynicism and action will overcome complacency. The feedback, recognition and satisfaction that come from being a Fred will fuel the continued effort.

The following brief chapters will remind you of four important basics for making the ordinary extraordinary. They are:

How to be a Fred

- MAKE A DIFFERENCE
- BUILD RELATIONSHIPS
- CREATE VALUE
- REINVENT YOURSELF

4 Make a Difference

> *The greatest things ever done on earth have been done little by little.*
>
> Thomas Guthrie
>
> *All men matter. You matter. I matter. It's the hardest thing in theology to believe.*
>
> G.K. Chesterton

I was in Cincinnati on a beautiful spring morning. I wasn't scheduled to speak until the afternoon, so I left my hotel and found a nearby coffee shop. After paying for a cup (free refills!), I took my newspaper outside to sit at the table by the sidewalk. For the next twenty minutes, I enjoyed reading and sipping.

A cab stand was just in front of where I was sitting. An older woman drove the second taxi in line. She got out to stretch and I noticed she was checking out the coffee shop. I didn't need to be clairvoyant to realize she was thinking about going inside. I got up and walked over to her. "Care for a cup of coffee?" I asked.

"That'd be great!" she replied.

"How do you take it?"

"Black." She was my kind of coffee drinker.

I went into the coffee shop, got my free refill and paid a little over a dollar for her cup. When I came back out she was digging in her pockets for change.

"Don't worry about it," I said, "the coffee is on me."

The last thing I recall before picking up my paper and heading back to the hotel was the look of amazement on her face.

That buck and change was the best money I spent that day. I was a Fred, which gave me a whole lot of satisfaction. And maybe I passed on some inspiration, too.

Did You Wake Up This Morning with the Intention to Change the World?

To admit that you begin the day planning to "change the world" certainly sounds grandiose (and perhaps a bit delusional). Yet I believe that you do change the world every day, whether you intend to or not. Often it only takes a little to make a big difference.

You change the world of your spouse or kids, depending on how you interact with them before you leave the house. A little extra time spent, a tender moment of affection or special attention changes their world that day. And it reminds you of what is important when the mad dash to the office irks you and makes you feel that the day is off to a rough start.

You change the world of another unknown driver when you allow him to change lanes without a blaring of horns, recognizing that he, too, is human and fallible. Of course you alter his world in a different way when you express anger with an obscene gesture.

You also change the worlds of a coworker, a customer, a vendor or a cafeteria worker by your demeanor.

The Fred Factor

No, these aren't dramatic changes. They won't determine the course of world affairs or affect a cure for AIDS. But who's to say that a myriad of these little changes don't have a cumulative affect in the lives of others that is truly profound?

Everybody Makes a Difference Every Day

You can read books on how to make a difference. You probably have heard teachers, pastors and speakers exhorting listeners to "make a difference."

The fact is, everybody already makes a difference every day. The real issue is what kind of difference are they making?

To make a difference means to affect another person, group or situation. It is nearly impossible to remain neutral as you travel through each day. Paying attention to others, giving them the respect they deserve, and serving them with a polite manner makes a positive difference.

In contrast, neglecting, criticizing and belittling others, whether intentionally or not, creates a negative difference.

The key is to pay attention to the kind of differences you make. You shouldn't be asking, "Did I make a difference today?" Of course you did! You undoubtedly affected somebody, maybe slightly, maybe significantly.

The most important question to ask yourself is: "What kind of difference did I make?"

As my friend and motorcycle riding buddy, Jim Cathcart, says, "To know more, notice more."

Make a Difference

Even Better Than Random Acts of Kindness

Maybe you've seen the bumper sticker "Practice Random Acts of Kindness." The idea is obvious: randomly do kind things for others. I certainly support that objective.

Just take it a step further

Why not "Practice Acts of the Extraordinary Regularly?"

Even the least "Fred-like" person can occasionally do something outstanding. When it happens, we should recognize it.

The purpose of this book is to help develop people who think, act and become Fred-like; they bring the same spirit of magnanimity to their work, relationships and life, not periodically, but persistently. They learn to look at the world through "Fred-colored glasses."

The things they do, both small and large, cumulatively create a lifestyle that becomes apparent to anybody paying the slightest attention. It's that kind of example that most influences others.

The Power of a Committed Individual

It's helpful to be reminded of how far-reaching our impact on others can be. A recent newspaper article proved that point powerfully to me.

In 1962, Dick Jordan was a rookie teacher at George Washington High School in Denver. He made sure to invite students to meet him on the first day of the millennium at the west entrance of the Denver Public Library Downtown. On the appointed day, nearly thirty years later, some three hundred students showed up.

Why, asked reporters, had they come? The answers were simple: they felt that Jordan cared for them. He taught them how to think, to question what was in history books, and in at least one case inspired a student to become a teacher. The husband of one student came because it was one of the last things his wife had asked as she was dying of cancer.

It had begun as a kind of joke. As a poor college graduate, Jordan had to borrow $300 from a Denver public schools recruiter just to make the trip to Colorado. He wore the same brown suit to school for three years.

He told his very first class, "I can retire in the year 2000—we ought to meet somewhere on that New Year's Day. And everybody bring a dollar, because I'm going to need it!"

His students remembered. The dollars they brought were donated to the Catholic Workers Soup Kitchen.

The Difference of a Great Idea

Bonnie McClurg understands how to make a difference. A reading teacher at Chandler Elementary School in Charleston, West Virginia, she changes lives, and she works with what she has.

Nine years ago, she observed that the students bought snacks from the school vending machine every day. This prompted her to think and take a leap forward: Why not make books as easy and inexpensive to buy as snack food? Quickly moving on her idea, she found a way to stock books alongside the pretzels and corn chips inside the machine.

Since then, students have been able to purchase books like *The Velveteen Rabbit* and *Amazing World of*

Dinosaurs for just fifty cents each, marked down from as much as $7.95. Is it any surprise that over 1,000 books have been purchased by eager students? Bonnie didn't sit on her idea; she made it happen. And she showed students that books can be enjoyable "snacks" too, ones that are always good for them.

Three Difference-Making Strategies

Continually create new ideas for how you'll make a difference

You'll be particularly interested in the ideas coming up in chapter six. I'll give you not only ideas and examples, but a way to think about making the ordinary extraordinary.

For now, it's important to raise awareness. Be vigilant not only for opportunities, but for ideas you can use...

Identify when you'll make a difference

My favorite answer to this question is "at every opportunity." Remember, nobody is forcing you to do extraordinary things. If your attempts at being a Fred become an oppressive duty, you're bound to fail. You're doing this, like most of the Freds I've encountered, because you want to and you can.

Target to whom you'll make a difference

Fred the Postman seems intent on providing exceptional service to all his customers. Is that possible for you and me? The answer, of course, is "it depends." I believe doing a great job for everyone you serve, at home or in business, is possible. Undoubtedly, there are those people you want to do something extraordinary for. The most important people in our lives deserve our best attention.

The Fred Factor

Customers: It would have been easy to write another book on customer service and use Fred the Postman as the primary illustration, but I wanted what I've learned from Fred and others like him to go beyond the marketplace and into every area of human relationships. But I acknowledge that perhaps the easiest application and quickest payoff is to begin by serving your customers like Fred served me. You'll instantly earn their attention and, soon, their unwavering devotion.

Family: How would your spouse react if you demonstrated Fred-like care and commitment to him or her? What about your kids? One of the saddest things in life is to know someone loves us but to rarely experience it. You can transform ordinary family interactions and events into extraordinary ideas by applying these principles at home.

Boss: Would you like to work for an incredible boss? Then start by treating your boss as incredible. Do extraordinary things for him or her, and over time I'll bet you'll notice a difference in your relationship. And if you don't, it's time to look for a new boss.

Teammates: High performance teams are made up of high performance teammates. Somebody has to go first—why not you? Become the Fred of your team or department and watch as the effect spreads to teammates.

Friends and Strangers: These aren't one and the same, of course, but the point is: what are you doing to enrich the lives of those you know, and those you don't? The only thing more fantastic than experiencing an "Act of Fred" from someone you know is when you experience it from a complete stranger. It restores one's faith in the potential of human behavior.

5   Build Relationships

> *Compared with what we ought to be, we are only half awake.*
>
> William James

One evening before my presentation at his sales conference, a vice president of sales for a large food products firm and I discovered that we were both big *motorheads* (car lovers).

"Do you read *AutoWeek*?" he asked. At the time I wasn't familiar with the publication but, after he told me about the magazine and what it covered, I made a mental note to subscribe to it.

My fellow motorhead was one step ahead of me. The next morning, before my speech, he handed me a subscription card that he had pulled out of his most recent issue.

I was struck by how thoughtful this small gesture was. As a result, I use a similar but amplified technique when I talk with friends and clients about books. If I find out that there is a really great title they've not read, I'll order a copy and have it sent to them with my compliments. That way, we both get a lot of satisfaction, and we also fortify our link and extend the range of our conversations and thoughts. That's quite a payoff for a simple act of relationship building!

Success is Built One Relationship at a Time

Every day we interact with dozens of people. Often, those interactions are fleeting and unmemorable. Freds, however, don't use people as a means to an end; they use relationships to build a foundation of success. They understand that all results are created by and through interactions with others. As a result, they become students of psychology. They understand that strong relationships create loyalty and are the basis of partnerships and teamwork. The best Freds build networks to develop distribution channels for their talents, and strive to work well with others, whether it's a one-on-one with a customer, or teamwork with colleagues.

The Dalai Lama and the Housekeeper

One morning after a public lecture, the Dalai Lama was walking back to his hotel room escorted by his usual entourage of admirers. Noticing a hotel employee standing nearby, he paused to talk with her. He inquired where she was from, and his genuine interest seemed to bring her out of her shyness. After a brief conversation, he departed, and the woman seemed truly excited by what had happened.

The next morning the Dalai Lama noticed the same housekeeper. She had brought a coworker with her and they both greeted him warmly. He responded in kind.

Each day, as he passed that way, he noticed more and more housekeepers waiting for a brief exchange with him. They formed a kind of receiving line leading to the elevator. A few moments of the Dalai Lama's time made a difference to the many gathered in the hallway.

Such is the excitement and appreciation a little attention can create. We want to be noticed and recognized as significant, and sometimes all it takes is a moment shared in the midst of another's busy schedule to remind us of our worth. Paying attention to another person pays off.

The Seven Bs of Relationship-Building

1. Be real

What made Fred the Postman so inspiring was his uniqueness. He was who he was. I never got the sense he was trying to impress me by being anybody but himself.

This is the direct opposite of the prevailing wisdom in our culture today, which is "fake it until you make it." The intent is to become who you want to be by acting like you were that person already. The only problem with that strategy is that you're a fake.

Try this alternative: always do your best being yourself. Aim to improve, try new things and add value. Let that come out of who you really are, what you truly believe in and the things you are committed to.

The prerequisite for relationship-building is trust. At the most basic level, trust is built on believing that someone is who he represents himself to be.

2. Be interested (not just interesting)

It may be true that interesting people attract attention, but I believe interested people attract appreciation. We like people who are interested in us.

When I first met Fred, he quickly introduced himself, but the focus was on how he could best help me meet my needs. I Instantly liked Fred because he showed a genuine interest in me, not because he was interesting (although, as I've learned over time, he certainly is). If Fred had spent time telling me what a great mailman he was, the outcome would have been different.

41

The Fred Factor

People are flattered when you express an interest in getting to know them better, not out of morbid curiosity, but in an effort to help or serve them better. Appreciating the people we serve, I believe, increases the value of our service to them.

3. Be knowledgeable by listening better

When you take an interest in people, they provide important information you can use to create value. For instance, if you learn that your boss hates to read long memos, you'll know that he will respond to, and be grateful for, a brief summary. Or, a lunch with a client reveals that she is seeking a new product because it concerns a subject that interests her fourteen year-old son. You find this out because you ask about her family—and listen to the response.

People are flattered when you make the effort to get to know them and seek information on how to serve them better. Understanding and appreciating what they want increases the value of what you can provide for them.

4. Be empathic

If you're interested in others and make the effort to truly understand them by listening, you'll be better able to appreciate how they feel. You may not always feel the same way—if you do, you are truly sympathetic—but when you can appreciate and understand how another feels, you are experiencing empathy. The need to be understood is one of the highest human needs, but too often the people in our lives either don't care or don't make the effort to understand how we really feel.

A wise man once said, "Be kind. everyone you meet is fighting a tough battle." His name was Philo Judaeus, and he said it 2,000 years ago. Not much has changed since, and his counsel is the essence of practical empathy.

5. Be honest

The real art of diplomacy isn't telling people what they want to hear; it's telling them what they need to know in such a way that they actually hear it. I summarize all business strategy into this simple idea: Say what you'll do, and do what you say. In other words, make no promises you can't keep. Don't create expectations you can't fulfill. Avoid over-representing and overpromising. Be a man, woman or organization of your word. That's integrity.

6. Be helpful

Little things make a big difference. Lots of small things cumulatively make a huge difference.

Years ago, I learned how to be of service to strangers from my friend Ken. If I see a group of people trying to get a picture taken by a member of their group, I offer to take the picture so that everybody can be included.

Even holding a door open is an indication of Fred-like behavior. So, remember your manners—and people will remember you.

7. Be prompt

Time is the one thing most people have far less of than disposable income. Giving people your attention—your time—is a great gift. Helping them save their time, by being prompt, efficient and fast, adds value to the ordinary. Relationships are based on the time spent on them, so make sure you give your best time.

6 *Creating Value*

> *There are two types of people who never achieve very much in their lifetimes. One is the person who won't do what he or she is told to do, and the other is the person who does no more than he or she is told to do.*
>
> Andrew Carnegie

The Most Valuable Skill: Adding Value to Everything.

A restaurateur was once asked the secret of his success. He said he had benefited from working in the kitchen of a great European restaurant. There he had learned that the key to greatness was to make everything as good as it could be, regardless of whether it was a complicated entrée or a simple side dish.

"If you serve French fries," he said, "make them the best French fries in the world."

Freds either create new value or add value to the work they do. At the same time, they know that something done, whether for a customer or colleague, that isn't valued could well be a waste of both time and energy.

Therefore, Freds compete successfully by offering better ideas, products and/or services than their competitors. They do more than talk about "value-added;" they deliver on it. The best are artists at taking ordinary job responsibilities, products and services and making them extraordinary. They are real-world alchemists who practice the art and science of value creation.

> Render more service than that for which you are paid and you will soon be paid for more than you render.
>
> Napoleon Hill

Freds create extra value by exceeding our expectations and doing more than is necessary, and often more than they're paid to do.

Once, I worked with a hospital that was committed to improving patient relations. One little idea made a big difference: whenever someone asked for directions, rather than simply telling them how to get where they wanted to go, the staff was encouraged to personally escort them, especially if they seemed confused or perplexed.

Anyone who has to go to a hospital, whether as a patient or as a visitor, is bound is be flummoxed. Having a personal escort relieves you of extra stress you don't need. The staff provided extra value by relieving a burden. It was beyond thoughtful; it was Fred-ful!

A Crash Course in Adding Value

1.Tell the truth

Truth seems to be in increasingly short supply. In the marketplace, we've become used to being told what others think we want to hear instead of what's really happening. An inquiry into delivery time gets a commitment for "first thing in the morning." By the end of the following day the package still hasn't arrived.

Truth telling should be a basic, not a value-added,

opportunity. A philosopher once commented that if honesty did not exist, someone would invent it as the best way of getting rich. Ironically, today truth is often so scarce that we assign an even higher value to it than we did in the past.

2. Practice personality power

I had just finished dining on the patio of one of my favorite Italian restaurants in Denver. My waitperson was nice, but not exceptional. I had observed an older gentleman who was filling water glasses and chatting with patrons. As I was paying my check, he approached to see if I needed a refill. His enthusiasm was genuine as he put his hand lightly on my shoulder and said "We're glad you came in today."

Those brief words brought an extraordinary conclusion to an otherwise unexceptional dining experience. What I had felt first-hand was the power of personality, of what happens when we extend ourselves to others genuinely and enthusiastically. This gentleman had turned filling water glasses and chatting into a fine art by injecting his own personality into the process.

3. Attract through Artistry

What are you doing to add an artistic flourish to your products or services? It can be as simple as a unique signature and as significant as a major improvement in packaging or design. We are drawn to attractiveness, not only in people, but in goods, services, architecture and all avenues of design.

Freds pay attention to appearances, not because they are more important than substance, but because they count. Something of great value unpleasantly presented diminishes in value. Conversely, we increase the value of things when we make them aesthetically pleasing.

4. Meet Needs In Advance

This is the power of anticipation. Have you ever rented a car, received directions to your destination, and then promptly become lost? Wouldn't it be a nice gesture at the rental counter if someone with a Fred-like mentality wrote down his or her direct dial number so you could call from your cell phone if you got lost?

5. Add "Good Stuff"

Think of your current position. Is there anything you could add to your teammates' or customers' experiences that would make their lives more enjoyable?

Here are three things to think about adding to your product, service or work:

Enjoyment: Ever wonder why most elevators have mirrors around them? It gives people something to do while waiting for the elevator! They get to admire themselves, check their grooming or discover the broccoli from lunch hanging off their chin. What can you do to add a little enjoyment to another's day?

I used to carry a bag of lollipops on airplanes for kids, flight attendants or anybody who wanted to indulge a sweet tooth. I have friends who know how to perform simple magic tricks. Sometimes they do it just to bring a smile to the face of another person. Sometimes they do magic to help close six figure sales. They know the power of adding a little good stuff, like enjoyment.

Enthusiasm: Think of enthusiasm as a blend of positive emotion and energy (this isn't a scientific or a dictionary definition). Enthusiasm is one of the primary ways that ordinary events, processes, services, or interactions become extraordinary.

Humor: Laughter is medicine for the soul. What product or service couldn't benefit from a spoonful of soul medicine? Even if your product or service is quite serious—and receiving your mail is, to most people, pretty serious business—you don't have to take yourself so seriously.

6. Subtract "Bad Stuff"

What annoys or irritates you? Wouldn't it be great if there was someone vigilant enough to notice what those irritants are, and to the degree they could reduce or eliminate them for you, they would?

That's what I mean by "subtract the bad stuff." Make it a point to notice, and then to reduce or eliminate, what others consider "the bad stuff."

Of course, one person's "bad stuff" isn't necessarily bad for another. It's important to know that the stuff you're subtracting is better gone.

What constitutes "bad stuff" (for most of us most of the time)?

Here are some of the most obvious of the baddest:

Waiting. Who likes to wait? Not many. While waiting can develop patience, most of us get far more practice than we'd prefer. Don't you love prompt people?

Don't you rejoice when your appointment starts, and ends, on time? Isn't it refreshing to see those people who provide service move with a sense of urgency, a sense of respect for your time. Freds are good at minimizing or eliminating the waiting their customers and colleagues experience.

Defects. Imperfection is the way of nature; nothing's perfect, that's true. But especially when we PAY for something to be "right" or "correct," it is maddening to experience an undeserved and unexpected flaw. A simple furniture delivery can go from excitement over a new piece of furniture to stewing over the fact that the desk is scratched on one end because of a careless move by the delivery person. Freds strive to make their work and services "defect free."

Mistakes. If defects happens to things, mistakes happen to processes. What a drag to have someone else make a mistake that you pay the consequences for ("I'm sorry ma'am, but somebody in our office lost your application. I'll have to ask you to send it in again...")

One of the most powerful things anybody can do to achieve Fred status is this: solve a problem that they didn't personally create.

How's that again?

Solve problems for people, even if you weren't responsible for the mistake ("I'm sorry ma'am, but someone in processing lost your application. I'll be glad to take the information by phone to minimize the time you spend reapplying...")

It's no compliment to be called a problem-spotter, but the world loves problem solvers. And Freds take responsibility for solving problems and mistakes, even if they didn't initially create them.

Irritation and Frustration. Can you really subtract those two negative emotions from another person? Indirectly, it is possible to start developing positive feelings in others.

I'd been getting the run around from the customer service department of an insurance company. I was so mad that I informed the principle that as soon as my policy expired, I wouldn't be doing business with his organization EVER AGAIN.

Evidently, he didn't pass on the information. When my policy expired, a woman named Theresa called me about replacing the policy through them.

I was incensed! "Doesn't the file say what a horrible, rotten experience I've had with your company?" I asked. "Do you have any idea how irritated and frustrated I've been trying to do business with you in the past?"

Theresa paused for a moment, then said, "I'm very sorry Mr. Sanborn. I don't know what you've experienced in the past here. But I promise you this: if you stay with us, I will personally service your account and you won't be disappointed again."

I did. And I wasn't.

Misinformation. Subtract as much of this stuff as you can. If you don't know, say so. And if there is a reason why you don't know, at least explain why that is and what you can offer in the way of accurate information.

While nobody likes bad news, there is something worse: good news that isn't exactly true. We get our hopes and expectations up when we get information from others only to have them dashed on the rocks of reality.

Truth-telling is, unfortunately, becoming scarce. We're told what others think we want to hear, not what we need to hear.

Get rid of misinformation.

7. Simplify

Make it easier for people to get what they need from you. Eliminate red-tape and mind-numbing bureaucracy. Don't break any laws or do anything immoral, but think about the systems you are a part of. You know how things work. Where are the shortcuts? What does an insider—that would be you—know that would benefit an outsider?

If you want to be of greater service to others, use your knowledge and expertise to help them understand what appears to be a complex and overwhelming situation.

If you were to call the help desk of a computer manufacturer because you were totally perplexed trying to set up your new computer, wouldn't you want to talk to a Fred? A Fred would probably begin by saying, "I know how confusing this looks, but I'm going to help you get up and running quickly..." and then would proceed to simplify the situation. A non-Fred might range from simply mechanical in their scripted responses to downright condescending.

8. Improve

To improve means to make better, a way of multiplying existing value. Do what you've always done, but do it better than you've ever done it. If you adopt that simple strategy, others will notice. In 1869, H.J. Heinz coined the goal of every Fred: "To do the common thing uncommonly well."

Think of all the uncommon things you could do uncommonly well. Would an extra sentence or two in an email make the difference between simply informative and truly helpful information? What kind of panache can you bring to your phone manner? Are you able to transform a phone complaint into another committed customer, not just because you addressed their problem, but because of the way you addressed it?

Freds are looking for ways, big and small, to improve upon their work.

9. Surprise

After hosting a large group of children and parents for our son Hunter's third birthday party, my wife and I were exhausted. We loaded up the Explorer with Grandma in tow and headed out for dinner. Our first two restaurants of choice had a wait, and we ended up at a Perkins restaurant by default. It epitomized "ordinary." The building was old, the interior needed an update and the menu was basic. The only thing surprising was the service.

Our waitperson was a relatively young woman with a cheerful demeanor. Taking our order and noticing the slumping adults while Hunter began to vocalize about his hunger, she promised to bring our food right out.

In a few minutes she was back with a stuffed Curious George monkey under her arm. My son loves Curious George. Our waitperson said, "I just won this stuffed animal and really don't have much use for it. I thought your son might enjoy it."

Hunter's face lit up as he accepted the unexpected gift. We thanked her and told her it was his birthday. "Well, happy birthday then!" she said and left to get our orders.

The food was pretty good and the bill was typical but the tip I left was exceptional, and she deserved it (although I really don't think that was her ulterior motive). A thoughtful gesture from a nice person had lifted all our spirits by her surprising gesture.

10. Entertain

"Gather 'round, one and all, watch and learn!" yelled the young man behind the marble table. "I am the King of Fudge!" For the next several minutes he narrated as he made a batch of fresh fudge, using a long paddle to mix and stir. The aroma was enticing, and the demonstration was impressive, but the overall effect was entertaining.

Let's be frank: if someone told me they wanted to go watch fudge being made, I'd pass on the invitation. But the King of Fudge knew something about human behavior that all Freds know: people love to be entertained. We pay closer attention, learn faster and are more engaged when we're being entertained.

I'm not talking about mindless entertainment. The King of Fudge had a reason for his performance: he wanted to sell more fudge. And he did.

7 Reinvent Yourself

> A disappointed man retired from his job,
>   Most days his work was like the day before.
> While not disliked, he won't be missed
>   He made good money, but still felt poor.
>
> He did what he was paid to do and nothing more,
>   But he never had much fun.
> He performed his job the way he lived his life:
>   The way it had always been done.

While not all change is good, it is also true that staying the same can't be all good either. The only difference between a rut and a grave, as the old saying goes, is the length.

Freds know that one of the most exciting things about life is that we awake each day with the ability to reinvent ourselves. No matter what happened yesterday, today is a new day. While we can't deny the struggles and setbacks, neither should we be restrained by them.

You've never been a Fred, you say? You're talking ancient history. That was yesterday. Today you can choose to be what you want to be. All you need to do is seize the opportunity to reinvent yourself.

If you hope to keep growing and going, you must reinvent yourself every day. Otherwise you'll fall behind in a competitive world.

1. Grow yourself, grow your value

The best way to add value is to begin by growing yourself. Become a sponge for ideas. Take time to truly think about what you do, and why you do it. So often we live our lives on autopilot, unable to distinguish between "activity" and "accomplishment."

The more you become, the more you'll have to share with others. Think of personal growth as the modeling material of reinvention. The more clay you have, the larger and more detailed a sculpture you can create. The more you learn—not abstract knowledge, but practical education—the more raw material you have for your own reinvention.

You increase in size as you increase your mental, spiritual and physical capabilities. As you grow, you'll make increasingly new connections with people and ideas that will enable you to become a master creator of value.

2. Be led by compelling reasons

It won't help much to be "driven" to reinvent yourself, and to improve on your best. The word suggests an almost unhealthy compulsion to do something because you should, not because you want to do it. Acting out of obligation is a good way to short-circuit what being a Fred is all about.

I don't know what motivated my postal carrier, Fred. I never had the opportunity to find out. I do know that he was doing an exceptional job because he wanted to, and he enjoyed it. How could I tell? By his demeanor. He was having fun, not complying with some work mandate.

Having a goal to become more Fred-like in your work won't motivate you; having compelling reasons—or a purpose—to become more Fred-like is where the motivation will come from. Those compelling reasons might range from the positive affect you'll have on others to the joy of doing an extraordinary job, to being a role model to inspire others. Whatever reason or reasons you identify, let them draw the best out of you.

3. Capitalize on your experiences

You've got a full life of experience. You've seen and experienced phenomenal things, and while you haven't exactly forgotten them, you rarely bring them into your conscious awareness.

If you want to reinvent yourself and improve for the future, spend some time reflecting on the past. What are the most important lessons you've learned? What did you once deeply desire to accomplish that you never attempted? Who are the people who most shaped your life, and what did you learn from them? Who do you admire the most, and what skills and characteristics that they possess would you like to develop in your life?

Buy a small journal. Jot down the answers to those questions. Add what you remember or learn each day. Capture the ideas that often stay hidden in the rich storehouse of your mind.

4. Increase your IQ

Of course, it isn't enough just to have good ideas if you don't do something with them.

IQ stands for implementation quotient. Intelligence Quotient supposedly measures what we know. Implementation Quotient measures what we do.

How many good ideas die for lack of action on your

part? Knowing you could have made someone's day and actually making their day are two dramatically different things.

One way to improve your IQ is to write down good ideas as they come to you, then put them on your daily "to do" list. Sometimes inaction is the result of a poor memory, and what's committed to writing is easier to remember and act upon.

5. Improve on the best

Seek out what the best are doing. Watch and learn. Then adapt and apply.

Good ideas are where you find them. If you just copied what everyone else was doing, you'd only do as well as everyone else is doing. The key is to adapt: to take good ideas from every source, and then apply them with your own special flair.

You can learn from the other Freds of the world: people in other departments within your organization, other organizations, industries or countries. While the ideas you observe may not be an exact fit for you, with some tailoring you can go beyond being simply emulative to being truly innovative.

6. Practice the One A Day Prescription

Good news: you don't have to do everything in an extraordinary manner. If you tried to do that, you'd get bogged down before you ever left home in the morning.

Turning the ordinary into the extraordinary is done one act at a time. If you did one extraordinary thing a day, whether at home or at work, seven days a week, 52 weeks a year (even while on vacation), your life would be a record book of the extraordinary.

One a day isn't overwhelming, but very doable. Dozens a day seems unrealistic, but one a day? Start by doing what you know you can do. As you continue reinventing yourself, supplement your "one a day strategy" by doing more. But build on that simple practice.

7.Compete Furiously... with Yourself!

It's common to compare ourselves with others. We want to know how we stack up, if we're better or worse. There's nothing inherently wrong with that, but it can be a crazy-maker. The reality: there will always be people accomplishing more than you, and there will always be people accomplishing less. The comparison game can be rigged simply by carefully choosing who or what you measure against.

It's a lot more fun to compare and compete against yourself. The goal is ongoing improvement—reinvention is positive change. Benchmark where you are against how far you've come and where you want to go.

The Ripple Effect

I had just finished speaking on the fifty-yard line of the Atlanta Georgia Dome. A group of one hundred highly creative techies (not an oxymoron) had gathered there for a department meeting. My speech seemed to be well received.

After talking with a few audience members, a man near the field entrance approached me. He extended his hand and said, "I'm one of the bus drivers. They didn't really invite us to attend your presentation, but I stood in the back anyway. I like hearing speakers and learning new ideas. I want you to know that you really encouraged me. You see,

I'm an inventor. I've invented a new seat cushion people can use when attending events in stadiums just like this one. And I agreed with practically everything you said. Your words have encouraged me to keep trying."

The client was very happy with my presentation that day. But the biggest reward came not from that, or the fee I received, but from the feedback of an appreciative individual who wasn't even supposed to be in the audience.

Is it possible that you are making significant impressions on others and don't ever know it? We need to be conscious of not only the primary effects of the things we do, but the secondary consequences, which are a ripple effect that touch people far beyond those in our immediate presence.

You just never know who's watching and listening. Our lives, to paraphrase Shakespeare, play out on a stage. We direct our words to a chosen audience. We need to remember that we wield a subtle power that can make significant differences to many outside our recognized audience. And sometimes the unintended consequences become the most valued of all.

Freds fulfill a passion for significance. They outlive themselves not by the results they've achieved, but by the way they've affected and touched others.

Bob Briner, president of ProServe and author of several books, including *Roaring Lambs*, distinguished himself by living a life of service. His trademark was to inquire with clients, friends and colleagues on how to he could serve them. It wasn't a hollow question: he worked hard to serve.

Just days before Bob succumbed to cancer, musician Michael Smith went to see him. Despite being weak and frail, Bob managed to ask his visitor one last question. It was "How can I serve you?"

Whether they are formal leaders, entrepreneurs or employees, Freds have a profound impact on others because of the example they set. Their efforts inspire, both directly and indirectly.

How to develop Freds

There are no less than two giant hardware stores known for their low prices within ten minutes of my house. Each have an amazing selection, but the service you receive when you shop there is ordinary.

That's why I rarely shop at either place.

Also ten minutes away is a smaller hardware store, probably 1/4 the size. While the pricing is competitive, I never expect the prices to be the lowest.

And I don't mind. Because the whole place is staffed with Freds.

I'm home-improvement challenged. I don't buy parts for the sprinkler system or washers for the plumbing, I buy answers to minor domestic crises.

When you walk into this hardware store, highly knowledgeable and helpful staff are near the door. If they don't have the answer to your question, they know the man or woman who does. They don't tell you where to find stuff, they take you to the exact spot. And they usually ask enough questions to find out if what you're trying to buy is what you really need.

While I can't recall any one person at this hardware store turning in the overall stellar performance of Fred the

Postman, I can tell you that this retailer is an example of what happens when you populate an organization with Fred-like employees.

Maybe that's one of the best kept secrets of competing successfully: Fred-like employees at every level in your organization.

How do you get them?

In an age of low unemployment, high turnover and nose-diving loyalty, developing Freds should be a critical priority for every business. Having Freds as teammates and leaders within your organization will distinguish the truly extraordinary company from the also-rans.

It is no secret that organizations have access to the same information, consultants, training, compensation systems, perks and benefits. Yet some soar while others flop. I'll risk the danger of oversimplification when I say that the difference is not in the things—processes, functions and structures—but in the people. Uninspired people rarely do inspired work.

Passionate people in an organization are different. They do ordinary things extraordinarily well. If their ideas are sometimes average, they are also useful. Occasionally, they are brilliant.

Customers don't have relationships with "organizations;" they form relationships with individuals. Passionate employees, whether they are salespeople, technicians or service reps, constantly show their commitment to customers. They do this by demonstrating their passion about what they do. As a result, Freds accomplish more than their blasé colleagues and are better able to meet the challenge of limited resources. Not surprisingly, they are also generally a happier lot because people doing good work feel good and people doing exceptional work feel, well, *exceptional*. Accomplishment contributes greatly to satisfaction.

How can you develop Freds? The next four chapters will spell it out:

Find
Reward
Educate
Demonstrate

Simple? Yes...

Easy? No...

But who ever said it would be easy to be extraordinary, or to develop extraordinary people?

8 Finding Freds

> There is something that is much more scarce, something finer by far, something rarer than ability. It is the ability to recognize ability.
>
> Elbert Hubbard

There are four basic ways to seek out Freds, both inside and outside of your organization.

1. Let them find you

Is your organization a Fred-magnet? If you really want your company to be world-class, it must become the kind of place that attracts Freds.

According to Dale Dauten, who wrote *The Gifted Boss*, people want to work in organizations—and for bosses—that give them a change and a chance.

The change is to work for an organization that recognizes, rewards, encourages and values Freds.

The chance is to become better than one has ever been.

In my opinion, these are what most Freds want and will seek.

Here's the catch: if you don't already have a number of living, breathing Freds doing exceptional things for your customers, your place of business isn't going to be perceived as the hot place to work. If your employees and colleagues don't go home at the end of the day and rave to family, friends and anybody who will listen about what a great company they work for, don't count on word of mouth to bring you a landslide of Fred-like applicants.

Sometimes you can acquire exceptional people from other departments in your own organization. They may be restrained by their current boss or situation, and looking for a place to "grow and show:" to develop their abilities and show what they're capable of doing.

Make your area a Fred oasis. I can't count the number of times really good department heads have told me that they got their best team players from other departments and managers that weren't taking good care of them.

2. Discover dormant Freds

Finding Freds is often no more difficult than uncovering the latent talent of those you already work with.

Remember when downsizing was so prevalent? Certainly some of it was necessary, but I've always felt much of it was a "quick fix." Managers believed it was easier to let employees go than to release their talents and abilities. What would have happened if managers took the time to uncover the hidden contributions employees could have made to justify their place in the organization?

Many employees are "loaded" for making the ordinary extraordinary, but nobody has figured out how to figuratively "pull the trigger."

Discovering talent is often nothing more than uncovering it. When you trust your people with the most valuable asset—time—to reveal their talents, you'll see just how many Freds there are in your organization

Finding Freds

Are there any tricks or techniques for spotting potential Freds? Philosophically, everyone has the potential to make the ordinary extraordinary. The kind of person I am referring to here is already inclined to do so. The most practical suggestion: pay attention. Watch for people who do things with flair (not to be confused with showing off or trying to attract attention). An exceptionally well-done project, an elegant client meeting or a clever suggestion are all possible tip-offs that there are more extraordinary abilities where those came from.

3. Hire them

What to ask the prospective Fred:

Who are your heroes? Why?
Why would anyone "do more than necessary?"
Tell me three things that you think would delight most customers.
What's the coolest thing that's happened to you as a customer?
What is service?

What to Ask Others About Them:

What do you remember most about _____?
What's the most extraordinary thing you remember this person doing?
How badly would they be missed if they left their current position?

Conclusion

There are lots of people like Fred "out there" in the marketplace. The challenge is finding them. The solution is to attract, uncover and hire them. All three are slightly different strategies, but each one compliments the other. Worked together, you can, over time, build a team of Freds.

9 *Reward*

> No man can become rich without himself
> enriching others.
>
> Andrew Carnegie

My friend, Dr. Michael LeBoeuf, in his insightful book *The Greatest Management Principle in the World,* sums it up quite neatly when he tells us we don't get the behavior we hope for, beg for or demand.

We get the behavior we reward.

The greatest management principle? What gets rewarded gets done. Michael then goes on to explain that it is a matter of rewarding the right behavior and using the right rewards.

The Atlanta Busboy

This instructive and touching story was related to me by Jim Cathcart, author of *The Acorn Principle*, and CEO of the Cathcart Institute, Inc. in La Jolla, CA.

A few years ago, I was travelling through the airport in Atlanta, Georgia. At the food court between concourses I stopped for a breakfast snack only to be confronted by thousands of fellow travelers also stopping to eat there. The place was packed! Every table had people standing nearby waiting to take over the seats on a moment's notice.

As I stood nearby, sipped my coffee and ate my muffin, I noticed a busboy cleaning the tables. He was sadly slumped over and looked defeated and depressed as he went about his work. He'd drag himself slowly from table to table, clearing the trash and wiping the tabletops. He made eye contact with no one and, as I watched him, I noticed that I was also becoming depressed!

I caught myself mid-emotion and said "somebody has to do something about this." So I did. I disposed of my trash and walked over to the busboy. I tapped him on the shoulder (which made him recoil as if he had been caught in a crime).

Then I said to him, "What you are doing here sure is important." He replied, "Huh?" I repeated myself and added, "If you weren't doing what you are doing, it wouldn't be five minutes before there was trash everywhere and people would stop coming in here. What you are doing is important and I just wanted to say thanks for doing it." Then I walked away. He was in shock. (Perhaps no one had ever spoken to him that way before.)

When I had walked about ten feet, I turned and looked back at him. In the time it took me to travel that distance, I could swear he had grown six inches! He was standing straighter, almost smiling and even looking some people in the eye. Now, he was not transformed into "Service Man," spreading cheer and goodwill. He was merely working a bit more effectively and no longer looking depressed.

What I had done was, in the overall scheme of things, trivial. My comments did not change the world... or did they? By simply pointing out how his behavior affected other people I had added dignity to his work. My simple acknowledgement of his worth had raised his opinion of himself in that role.

When one doesn't see much meaning in what one does, one won't bring much value to what one does.

Not only that: In the course of that workday, that busboy probably came into contact with hundreds of people, all of whom were traveling somewhere to interact with still others. Now, instead of a gloomy experience, they had a more pleasant interaction with this busboy.

Intention Counts, Too

It's just as important to reward intention as much as outcome. While no one likes to fail, it is much more important to know that taking chances will be acknowledged—and not punished. Nobody hits a home run every time. (As a matter of fact, home run hitters tend to strike out more than other batters.) When people feel that their contribution is worthless they will stop trying. And when that happens, innovation dies.

Make It So

Take a good look around your division. Rewarding employees is not hard to do. All you have to do, on a consistent basis, is make sure that:

● Everyone on your team knows that he or she is making an important contribution, or has the ability to.

● Tell them what kind of difference they are making. Be specific. Cite increased production, sales, hires, commendations from outside sources, insightful suggestions—anything and everything that applies.

● Be sure that positive feedback about their efforts is a rule—not an exception.

● Create an award. Consider a trophy or a plaque, and even a small monetary amount. Don't make the value of the award so large in monetary terms that it looks like a Fred-bribe. Have fun sharing tangible recognition. Consider giving multiple Fred awards each month if several people are deserving.

● Get the leader (president, director, etc.) of your organization to personally recognize those who contribute like Fred. Ask him or her to send a note, or make a phone call to let the employee know their contribution has been noticed and appreciated.

Remember the reward formula and apply it often: recognize a contribution, reinforce how it affects your business, and repeat. Praise for trying—both written and spoken frequently in public and in private—are the best rewards.

10   *Educate*

> *Who dares to teach must never cease to learn.*
> John Cotton Dana,
> motto of Kean College, New Jersey
>
> *The brighter you are, the more you have to learn.*
> Don Herold
>
> *The chief object of education is not to learn things but to unlearn things.*
> G.K. Chesterton

Whether or not they embrace the language I've used throughout this book, management and leadership universally embrace the concepts, or at least say that they do. Curiously, I rarely, if ever, see managers or organizations attempting to teach the principles embodied by The Fred Factor.

Part of this philosophy is about having fun. That's what makes work interesting and exciting, not only for the people doing the work, but for customers and coworkers as well.

In the spirit of fun, you could call this chapter "Providing a Freducation." Of course it would ruin the FRED acronym I've been working from, but what I'm really suggesting is to consciously teach people ways to think and perform like Fred.

An unexpected benefit of teaching these things is that

it will make you a better manager or leader; you'll increase your Freducation—your skillset—in the process.

1. Find Examples Everywhere

What do you notice when you're on vacation? If you're a photographer, you probably have a greater awareness of photo opportunities. If you're a musician, you most likely pay closer attention to the musical style of the location. In other words, your interests focus your awareness.

As you become increasingly interested in developing the art of the extraordinary in yourself and others, you'll notice more and more examples. Not only will you see little things done in exceptional ways, and notice people who make the extra effort to be extraordinary, but you'll also notice "anti-Fred" examples as well. You'll think, "Here's a great example of what not to do!"

Record those ideas and examples. Write them down. If you run across them in your reading, highlight them. Clip out newspaper articles. Put all these examples in a Fred File, and you'll have some of the best training illustrations imaginable. Why? Because they're real life, not abstract or contrived. Nothing inspires people more than an example directly experienced or indirectly learned.

Challenge the people on your team to collect examples as well. Begin or end meetings with the question, "Who's got a Fred example to share?" Make it a friendly contest with a nominal award. Maybe even post the "example of the week" where others can see it as well.

2. Dissect and debrief

Generally, a change doesn't stick unless we understand why it happened. Even the best examples can lose impact if we don't take time to consider why they worked.

Dissecting and debriefing is a way of accomplishing four things: 1) identifying the specific good idea behind the example, 2) adapting it to your situation 3) looking for ways to improve it and 4) identifying opportunities to apply it.

The good idea: How did that make you feel? What makes that example cool? Or what makes that an example of what not to do? What's the basic idea here?

Adapting it to your situation: Would that work for us? How could it work for us? What would we have to do, or do differently, to benefit from this example?

Looking for ways to improve it: What would make this even better? What would you do differently? What would make our customers appreciate this even more?

Opportunities for application: When do you see using this idea? Where? With whom? When will you start?

3. Teach Miracle Working

My friend and fellow speaker, Don Hutson, has an important insight about "miracles" that individuals and organizations are able to pull off for customers. He asks, "When do these miracles usually happen?" The answer: when there's a crisis. There's nothing like a crisis to get our attention and make us perform beyond our present capabilities.

But that's not the point. Don's message is more important: Don't wait for a crisis! Perform miracles on a regular basis. He also correctly identifies that most of these "miracles" are performed by an individual with a big heart and a caring spirit. That's an extremely accurate description of the kind of person who understands the Fred Factor.

Educate

Do you expect miracle working on a regular basis? Or do you reserve such extraordinary performance for a crisis? Teach the Fred Factor as a form of daily miracle working (the size of the miracle is less important than it's frequency).

4. Pull, don't push

You can't command someone to be a Fred. You can't require someone to practice the Fred Factor. You can try, of course. But it won't work. Command-and-control short-circuits the spirit of the Fred Factor. It's about opportunity, not obligation.

Here's what you can do: Invite people to join you. In other words, pull, don't push. Use your enthusiasm and commitment to gain their participation and involvement.

The most powerful tool you have for spreading the Fred Factor throughout your organization is your own behavior, and that's the subject of the next chapter.

11 Demonstrate

> *You can preach a better sermon with your life than your lips.*
> Oliver Goldsmith

Think of a friend or acquaintance who inspires you by his or her example.

I have a friend who lives in a city my wife and I often visit to see relatives. He is, in my mind, the epitome of the southern gentleman. A highly successful businessman with exceptional taste, his home and furnishings are impressive, and he owns and pilots his own airplane. Yet, despite the outer trappings of success, he is a most humble and sincere human being.

Whenever I'm in his town I make it a point to have lunch with him. Whenever he hears that I am coming he always asks me, "Is there anything I can do for you while you're here?"

Isn't that the essential question the Freds of the world ask, either aloud or silently, of the people they serve?

Some might ask that question superficially, but I know from my friend's character and behavior that he is completely serious. If I said I needed a car to get around, I know with certainty he'd lend me one of his, or find one I could borrow. That's the kind of person that he is.

But my friend does more than offer to extend himself

to make my visit more enjoyable. He inspires me to act simi-larly, to strive to be the kind of person that he is. While he's never coached or counseled me on how to be of greater service, or how to be what I've called more "Fred-like," he has done as much or more to instill that desire within me as anyone I've met.

He inspires me with the example of his life.

The Magic Question

How could you inspire your employees to serve your customers, vendors and fellow employees better by example? There are four simple rules to follow.

1. Inspire...

...but don't intimidate.

When I share the story of Fred the Postman with audiences, the best reaction I get goes something like this: "Cool! I could do that, too!"

If Fred came across as super-human or inherently extraordinary, he wouldn't inspire people, he'd intimidate them.

Fred inspired me because, like you and me, he's an ordinary guy, doing an extraordinary job.

Your example should be doable and down-to-earth. If you come across as genetically engineered for exceptional performance, others who lack the DNA will opt out of even trying.

2. Involve

The Fred Factor

Here's a radical idea: TEAM FRED. There's no rule that says a team can't harness and benefit from the Fred Factor.

Many years ago, a buddy invited me to join him in doing something nice at Thanksgiving. The year before he'd found out about a family that couldn't afford a nice Thanksgiving dinner, so he purchased all the fixings and delivered it to their home the day before.

This year he invited me to join him. Wow! It was a neat thing to do, and I've since invited others to join me in similar activities.

That's the power of involvement. It's far more effective than suggesting or asking.

What can you do to involve others in purposeful acts of Fredness?

3. Initiate

Don't wait for "the right moment." It will never come.

Don't wait until somebody else goes first. Maybe they will. Probably they won't.

Don't wait for the perfect opportunity. Just take an opportunity and make it perfect.

You can set the pace for extraordinary performance in your organization, but only if you initiate. That means taking action. Boldly. Quickly.

Be humble in your motive, but not in your example. Don't do it for the recognition, do it to create participation. You become the spark that sets the place on fire when you initiate.

4. Improvise

If I were going to give you a homework assignment for both learning and teaching the Fred Factor, it might be to attend an improv comedy performance. The beauty of improv is that it proves you can make just about any circumstance or situation funny. As in life, the situation doesn't determine the outcome, the participants do.

Take what life gives you. You might become a positive example not because of your situation, but in spite of it! You may have the most dead-end job on the planet, but that shouldn't keep you from reinventing yourself and your job. In the process of improvising—trying stuff to see what works—you'll probably improve your job (or relationship or situation). And, hey, even if you don't, at least you won't be bored anymore!

Forget what you've heard about "those who can, do, and those who can't teach." Not only is it derogatory to the dedicated professionals in education and training, but with a few exceptions, it just ain't so.

The reality? Those that do best teach best. The man or woman who can demonstrate the lesson with his or her life most powerfully impacts others.

When those who know are able to show, those who learn are able to grow. And that's what a good Freducation is all about.

Conclusion

> *At the Day of Judgment we shall not be asked what we have read but what we have done.*
> Thomas à Kempis

Three Final Ideas to Spread Fred

1. Recognize the Freds in your life.

Reflect back over your life. Who have been the Freds? The relatives, teachers, pastors, rabbis, friends and others who have made the biggest difference in your life?

Maybe it was somebody you encountered in your business yesterday. Whoever, and whenever, don't take lightly the extraordinary things people have done and do for you.

2. Acknowledge them for their contribution.

Once you realize who the Freds in your life have been, make time to let them know how much you appreciate it. Write them a letter or a note. Send them a gift. Write an article or letter to the editor, and make sure they get a copy. Nominate them for a Fred Award (www.fredfactor.com) Just make sure they know they are valued and appreciated.

3. Pay them back by becoming a Fred, too.

The only thing better than an acknowledgement is action. Choose to do something extraordinary and dedicate it to someone who inspired you. The best payback, as the popular book says, is to "pay it forward."

Fred has already become a chain reaction, first in my life and in the lives of his customers. Now he has affected hundreds, if not thousands, as I've shared his story. Think of the people who must have had a positive impact on Fred the Postman. The chain reaction was begun long before Fred started delivering mail on my street.

Using the Fred Factor won't cure the common cold or create world peace, but it will warm the lives of many and create peace in their corner of the world.

Isn't it great knowing you have the ability to do that?

About the Author

Mark Sanborn is known internationally as "the high content speaker who motivates." He presents 90-100 programs every year on leadership, team building, customer service and mastering change. He is president of Sanborn & Associates, Inc., an idea lab dedicated to developing leaders in business and in life.

Mark's client list includes Exxon, Airtouch Cellular, BMW Financial, Mortons of Chicago, New York Life, Price Costco, ServiceMaster, and Hewlett Packard.

Presentations magazine featured Mark in 1995 as one of five "Masters of the Microphone." Mark holds the Certified Speaking Professional designation and is one of the youngest speakers ever inducted into the Speaker Hall of Fame. He is also a member of the exclusive Speakers Roundtable, a group of twenty of the world's top speakers.

Mark is also the author or coauthor of nine books, including *Teambuilt: Making Teamwork Work*, *Sanborn On Success*, *Best Practices In Customer Service*, and *Meditations for the Road Warrior*. He has created and appeared in twenty videos and numerous audio training programs. And he's a founding professor of MentorU.com, an Internet-based knowledge transfer company.

Visit the Fred Factor website at www.FredFactor.com.

Contact Mark Sanborn at 1-800-650-3343.